A Treatise Concerning Man's Perfection in Righteousness

A Treatise Concerning Man's Perfection in Righteousness

St. Augustine

A Treatise Concerning Man's Perfection in Righteousness

© Lighthouse Publishing 2018

Written by: St. Augustine (Nov.13 354 – Aug.28 430)
Translated by Peter Holmes and Robert Ernest Wallis
Revised by: Professor Benjamin B. Warfield, D.D
Updated into Modern U.S English by A.M. Overett (b. 1960)

All rights reserved. Without limiting the rights under copyright reserved above, no part of this publication may be reproduced, stored in a retrieval system, or transmitted, in any form or by any means (electronic, mechanical, photocopying, recording or otherwise), without the prior written permission of the copyright owner of this book.

Published by
Lighthouse Christian Publishing
SAN 257-4330
5531 Dufferin Drive
Savage, Minnesota, 55378
United States of America

www.lighthousechristianpublishing.com

PREFACE TO THE TREATISE ON MAN'S PERFECTION IN RIGHTEOUSNESS.

Augustin has made no mention of this treatise in his book of Retractations; for the reason, no doubt, that it belonged to the collection of the Epistles, for which he designed a separate statement of Retractations. In all the mss. this work begins with his usual epistolary salutation: "Augustin, to his holy brethren and fellow-bishops Eutropius and Paulus." And yet, by general consent, this epistle has been received as a treatise, not only in those volumes of his works which contain this work, but also in the writings of those ancient authors who quote it. Amongst these, the most renowned and acquainted with Augustin's writings, Possidius (In indiculo, 4) and Fulgentius (Ad Monimum, i. 3) expressly call this work "A Treatise on the Perfection of Man's Righteousness." So far nearly all the mss. agree, but a few (including the Codd. Audöenensis and Pratellensis) add these words to the general title: "In opposition to those who assert that it is possible for a man to become righteous by his own sole strength." In a ms. belonging to the Church of Rheims there occurs this inscription: "A Treatise on what are called the definitions of Cœlestius." Prosper, in his work against the Collator, ch. 43, advises his reader to read, besides some other of Augustin's "books," that which he wrote "to the priests Paulus and Eutropius in opposition to the questions of Pelagius and Cœlestius."

From this passage of Prosper, however, in which he mentions, but with no regard to accurate order, some of the short treatises of Augustin against the Pelagians, nobody could rightly show that this work On the

Perfection of Man's Righteousness was later in time than his work On Marriage and Concupiscence, or than the six books against Julianus, which are mentioned previously in the same passage by Prosper. For, indeed, at the conclusion of the present treatise, Augustin hesitates as yet to censure those persons who affirmed that men are living or have lived in this life righteously without any sin at all: their opinion Augustin, in the passage referred to (just as in his treatises On Nature and Grace, n. 3, and On the Spirit and the Letter, nn. 49, 70), does not yet think it necessary stoutly to resist. Nothing had as yet, therefore, been determined on this point; nor were there yet enacted, in opposition to this opinion, the three well-known canons (6–8) of the Council of Carthage, which was held in the year 418. Afterwards, however, on the authority of these canons, he cautions people against the opinion as a pernicious error, as one may see from many passages in his books Against the two Epistles of the Pelagians, especially Book iv. ch. x. (27), where he says: "Let us now consider that third point of theirs, which each individual member of Christ as well as His entire body regards with horror, where they contend that there are in this life, or have been, righteous persons without any sin whatever." Certainly, in the year 414, in an epistle (157) to Hilary, when answering the questions which were then being agitated in Sicily, he expresses himself in the same tone, and almost in the same language, on sinlessness, as that which he employs at the end of this present treatise. "But those persons," says he (in ch. ii. n. 4 of that epistle), "however much one may tolerate them when they affirm that there either are, or have been, men besides the one Saint of saints who have been wholly free from sin; yet when they allege that man's own free will is sufficient for fulfilling the Lord's commandments, even when unassisted by God's grace and the gift of the Holy Spirit for the performance of good works, the idea is altogether worthy of anathema and of perfect detestation." On comparing these words with the conclusion of this treatise before us, nothing will appear more probable than that the work which supplies the refutation of Cœlestius' questions, which were also brought over from Sicily, was written not long after the above-mentioned epistle. This work Possidius, in his index, places immediately after the treatise On Nature and Grace, and before the book On the Proceedings of Pelagius. Augustin, however, does not mention this work in his epistle (169) which he addressed to Evodius about the end of the year 415; but he intimates in it that he had published an answer to the Commonitorium of Orosius, wherein that author stated that "the bishops Eutropius and Paulus had already given information to Augustin about certain formidable heresies." Some suppose that this statement refers to the letter which they dispatched to Augustin along with Cœlestius' propositions. However, that be, it is not unreasonable to believe that they, not long after Orosius' arrival in Africa (that is, before the midsummer of the year 415), had sent these propositions to him, and that Augustin soon afterwards wrote back to Eutropius and Paulus a refutation of them, his answer to Orosius having been previously given.

Furthermore, Cœlestius, whose name is inscribed in the propositions, "wrote to his parents from his monastery," as Gennadius informs us in his work on Church writers (De Scriptoribus Ecclesiasticis), "before he fell in with the teaching of Pelagius, three letters in the shape of short treatises, necessary for all seekers after

God." Afterwards he openly professed the Pelagian heresy, and published a short treatise, in which, besides other topics, he acknowledged in the Church of Carthage that even infants had redemption by being baptized into Christ,—an episcopal decision on the question having been obtained in that city about the commencement of the year 412, as we learn from an epistle to Pope Innocent (amongst the Epistles of Augustin [175, n. 1 and 6]), as well as from the epistle [157, n. 22] which we have referred to above; and from Augustin's work On the Merits of Sins, i. 62, and ii. 59; also from his treatise On Original Sin, 21; and his work Against Julianus, iii. 9. Another work by an anonymous writer, but which was commonly attributed to Cœlestius, divided into chapters, is mentioned in the treatise which follows the present one, On the Proceedings of Pelagius; see chapters 29, 30, and 62. There were extant, moreover, in the year 417, several small books or tracts of Cœlestius, which Augustin, in his work On the Grace of Christ, 31, 32, and 36, says were produced by Cœlestius himself in some ecclesiastical proceedings at Rome under Zosimus. Augustin, at the commencement of the present work On the Perfection of Man's Righteousness, mentions an undoubted work of Cœlestius as having been seen by him, from which he discovered that the definitions or propositions therein examined by Augustin were not unsuited to the tone and temper of Cœlestius. This was very probably the book which Jerome quotes in his Epistle to Ctesiphon, written in the year 413 or 414. These are Jerome's words: "One of his followers [that is, Pelagius'], who was already in fact become the master and the leader of all that army, and 'a vessel of wrath,'[1361]in opposition to the apostle, runs on through thickets, not of syllogisms, as his admirers are apt to boast, but of solecisms, and philosophizes and disputes to the following effect: 'If I do nothing without God's help, and if everything which I shall achieve is owing to His operations solely, then it follows that it is not I who work, but only God's work is to be crowned in me. In vain, therefore, has He conferred on me the power of will, if I am unable to exercise it fully without His incessant help. That volition, indeed, is destroyed which requires the assistance of another. But it is free will which God has given to me; and free it can only remain, if I do whatever I wish. The state of the case then is this: I either use once for all the power which has been bestowed on me, so that free will is preserved; or else, if I require the assistance of another, liberty of decision in me is destroyed.'"

A TREATISE CONCERNING MAN'S PERFECTION IN RIGHTEOUSNESS,

BY AURELIUS AUGUSTIN, BISHOP OF HIPPO;

In One Book, addressed to Eutropius and Paulus, a.d.415.

A paper containing sundry definitions, said to have been drawn up by Cœlestius, was put into the hands of Augustin. In this document, Cœlestius, or some person who shared in his errors, had recklessly asserted that a man had it in his power to live here without sin. Augustin first refutes the several propositions in brief answers, showing that the perfect and plenary state of righteousness, in which a man exists absolutely without sin, is unattainable without grace by the mere resources of our corrupt nature, and never occurs in this present state of existence. He next proceeds to consider the authorities which the paper contained as gathered out of the Scriptures; some of them teaching man to be "unspotted" and "perfect;" others mentioning the commandments of God as "not grievous;" while others again are quoted as opposed to the authoritative passages which the Catholics were accustomed to advance against the Pelagians.

Chapter I.

Your love, which in both of you is so great and so holy that it is a delight to obey its commands, has laid me under an obligation to reply to some definitions which are said to be the work of Cœlestius; for so runs the title of the paper which you have given me, "The definitions, so it is said, of Cœlestius." As for this title, I take it that it is not his, but theirs who have brought this work from Sicily, where Cœlestius is said not to be, —although many there make boastful pretension of holding views like his, and, to use the apostle's word, "being themselves deceived, lead others also astray." That these views are, however, his, or those of some associates of his, we, too, can well believe. For the above-mentioned brief definitions, or rather propositions, are by no means at variance with his opinion, such as I have seen it expressed in another work, of which he is the undoubted author. There was therefore good reason, I think, for the report which those brethren, who brought these tidings to us, heard in Sicily, that Cœlestius taught or wrote such opinions. I should like, if it were possible, so to meet the obligation imposed on me by your brotherly kindness, that I, too, in my own answer should be equally brief. But unless I set forth also the propositions which I answer, who will be able to form a judgment of the value of my answer? Still I will try to the best of my ability, assisted, too, by God's mercy, by your own prayers, so to conduct the discussion as to keep it from running to an unnecessary length.

Chapter II. — (1.) The First Breviate of Cœlestius.

I. "First of all," says he, "he must be asked who denies man's ability to live without sin, what every sort of sin is, —is it such as can be avoided? or is it unavoidable? If it is unavoidable, then it is not sin; if it can be avoided, then a man can live without the sin which can be avoided. No reason or justice permits us to designate as sin what cannot in any way be avoided." Our answer to this is, that sin can be avoided, if our corrupted nature be healed by God's grace, through our Lord Jesus Christ. For, in so far as it is not sound, in so far does it either through blindness fail to see, or through weakness fail to accomplish, that which it ought to do; "for the flesh lusted against the spirit, and the spirit against the flesh," so that a man does not do the things which he would.

(2.) The Second Breviate.

II. "We must next ask," he says, "whether sin comes from will, or from necessity? If from necessity, it is not sin; if from will, it can be avoided." We answer as before; and in order that we may be healed, we pray to Him to whom it is said in the psalm: "Lead Thou me out of my necessities."

(3.) The Third Breviate.

III. "Again we must ask," he says, "what sin is, — natural? or accidental? If natural, it is not sin; if accidental, it is separable; and if it is separable, it can be avoided; and because it can be avoided, man can be without that which can be avoided." The answer to this is, that sin is not natural; but nature (especially in that corrupt state from which we have become by nature "children of wrath") has too little determination of will to avoid sin, unless assisted and healed by God's grace through Jesus Christ our Lord.

(4.) The Fourth Breviate.

IV. "We must ask, again," he says, "What is sin,

—an act, or a thing? If it is a thing, it must have an author; and if it be said to have an author, then another besides God will seem to be introduced as the author of a thing. But if it is impious to say this, we are driven to confess that every sin is an act, not a thing. If therefore it is an act, for this very reason, because it is an act, it can be avoided." Our reply is, that sin no doubt is called an act, and is such, not a thing. But likewise in the body, lameness for the same reason is an act, not a thing, since it is the foot itself, or the body, or the man who walks lame because of an injured foot, that is the thing; but still the man cannot avoid the lameness, unless his foot be cured. The same change may take place in the inward man, but it is by God's grace, through our Lord Jesus Christ. The defect itself which causes the lameness of the man is neither the foot, nor the body, nor the man, nor indeed the lameness itself; for there is of course no lameness when there is no walking, although there is nevertheless the defect which causes the lameness whenever there is an attempt to walk. Let him therefore ask, what name must be given to this defect, —would he have it called a thing, or an act, or rather a bad property in the thing, by which the deformed act comes into existence? So in the inward man the soul is the thing, theft is an act, and avarice is the defect, that is, the property by which the soul is evil, even when it does nothing in gratification of its avarice, even when it hears the prohibition, "Thou shalt not covet," and censures itself, and yet remains avaricious. By faith, however, it receives renovation; in other words, it is healed day by day, —yet only by God's grace through our Lord Jesus Christ.

Chapter III. — (5.) The Fifth Breviate.

V. "We must again," he says, "inquire whether a man ought to be without sin. Beyond doubt he ought. If he ought, he is able; if he is not able, then he ought not. Now if a man ought not to be without sin, it follows that he ought to be with sin, —and then it ceases to be sin at all, if it is determined that it is owed. Or if it is absurd to say this, we are obliged to confess that man ought to be without sin; and it is clear that his obligation is not more than his ability." We frame our answer with the same illustration that we employed in our previous reply. When we see a lame man who has the opportunity of being cured of his lameness, we of course have a right to say: "That man ought not to be lame; and if he ought, he is able." And yet whenever he wishes he is not immediately able; but only after he has been cured by the application of the remedy, and the medicine has assisted his will. The same thing takes place in the inward man in relation to sin which is its lameness, by the grace of Him who "came not to call the righteous, but sinners;" since "the whole need not the physician, but only they that be sick."

(6.) The Sixth Breviate.

VI. "Again," he says, "we have to inquire whether man is commanded to be without sin; for either he is not able, and then he is not commanded; or else because he is commanded, he is able. For why should that be commanded which cannot at all be done?" The answer is, that man is most wisely commanded to walk with right steps, on purpose that, when he has discovered his own inability to do even this, he may seek the remedy which is provided for the inward man to cure the lameness of sin, even the grace of God, through our Lord Jesus Christ.

(7.) The Seventh Breviate.

VII. "The next question we shall have to propose," he says, "is, whether God wishes that man be without sin. Beyond doubt God wishes it; and no doubt he has the ability. For who is so foolhardy as to hesitate to believe that to be possible, which he has no doubt about God's wishing?" This is the answer. If God wished not that man should be without sin, He would not have sent His Son without sin, to heal men of their sins. This takes place in believers who are being renewed day by day, until their righteousness becomes perfect, like fully restored health.

(8.) The Eighth Breviate.

VIII. "Again, this question must be asked," he says, "how God wishes man to be, —with sin, or without sin? Beyond doubt, He does not wish him to be with sin. We must reflect how great would be the impious blasphemy for it to be said that man has it in his power to be with sin, which God does not wish; and for it to be denied that he has it in his power to be without sin, which God wishes: just as if God had created any man for such a result as this,—that he should be able to be what He would not have him, and unable to be what He would have him; and that he should lead an existence contrary to His will, rather than one which should be in accordance therewith." This has been in fact already answered; but I see that it is necessary for me to make here an additional remark, that we are saved by hope. "But hope that is seen is not hope; for what a man sees, why doth he yet hope for? But if we hope for that we see not, then do we with patience wait for it." Full righteousness, therefore, will only then be reached, when fulness of health is attained; and this fulness of health shall be when there is fulness of love, for "love is the fulfilling of the law;" and then shall come fulness of love, when "we shall see Him even as He is." Nor will any addition to love be possible more, when faith shall have reached the fruition of sight.

Chapter IV. — (9.) The Ninth Breviate.

IX. "The next question we shall require to be solved," says he, "is this: By what means is it brought about that man is with sin? —by the necessity of nature, or by the freedom of choice? If it is by the necessity of nature, he is blameless; if by the freedom of choice, then the question arises, from whom he has received this freedom of choice. No doubt, from God. Well, but that which God bestows is certainly good. This cannot be gainsaid. On what principle, then, is a thing proved to be good, if it is more prone to evil than to good? For it is more prone to evil than to good if by means of it man can be with sin and cannot be without sin." The answer is this: It came by the freedom of choice that man was with sin; but a penal corruption closely followed thereon, and out of the liberty produced necessity. Hence the cry of faith to God, "Lead Thou me out of my necessities." With these necessities upon us, we are either unable to understand what we want, or else (while having the wish) we are not strong enough to accomplish what we have come to understand. Now it is just liberty itself that is promised to believers by the Liberator. "If the Son," says He, "shall make you free, ye shall be free indeed." For, vanquished by the sin into which it fell by its volition, nature has lost liberty. Hence another scripture says, "For of whom a man is overcome, of the same is he brought in bondage." Since therefore "the whole need not the physician, but only they that be sick;" so likewise it is not the free that need the Deliverer, but only the enslaved. Hence the cry of joy to Him for deliverance, "Thou hast saved my soul from the straits of necessity." For true liberty is also real health; and this would never have been lost, if the will had remained good. But because the will has sinned, the hard necessity of having sin has pursued the sinner; until his infirmity be wholly healed, and such freedom be regained, that there must needs be, on the one hand, a permanent will to live happily, and, on the other hand, a voluntary and happy necessity of living virtuously, and never sinning.

(10.) The Tenth Breviate.

X. "Since God made man good," he says, "and, besides making him good, further commanded him to do good, how impious it is for us to hold that man is evil, when he was neither made so, nor so commanded; and to deny him the ability of being good, although he was both made so, and commanded to act so!" Our answer here is: Since then it was not man himself, but God, who made man good; so also is it God, and not man himself, who remakes him to be good, while liberating him from the evil which he himself did upon his wishing, believing, and invoking such a deliverance. But all this is affected by the renewal day by day of the inward man, by the grace of God through our Lord Jesus Christ, with a view to the outward man's resurrection at the last day to an eternity not of punishment, but of life.

Chapter V.— (11.) The Eleventh Breviate.

XI. "The next question which must be put," he says, "is, in how many ways all sin is manifested? In two, if I mistake not: if either those things are done which are forbidden, or those things are not done which are commanded. Now, it is just as certain that all things which are forbidden can be avoided, as it is that all things which are commanded are able to be affected. For it is vain either to forbid or to enjoin that which cannot either be guarded against or accomplished. And how shall we deny the possibility of man's being without sin, when we are compelled to admit that he can as well avoid all those things which are forbidden, as do all those which are commanded?" My answer is, that in the Holy Scriptures there are many divine precepts, to mention the whole of which would be too laborious; but the Lord, who on earth consummated and abridged His word, expressly declared that the law and the prophets hung on two commandments, that we might understand that whatever else has been enjoined on us by God ends in these two commandments, and must be referred to them: "Thou shalt love the Lord thy God with all thy heart, and with all thy soul, and with all thy mind;" and "Thou shalt love thy neighbor as thyself." "On these two commandments," says He, "hang all the law and the prophets." Whatever, therefore, we are by God's law forbidden, and whatever we are bidden to do, we are forbidden and bidden with the direct object of fulfilling these two commandments. And perhaps the general prohibition is, "Thou shalt not covet;"

and the general precept, "Thou shalt love." Accordingly the Apostle Paul, in a certain place, briefly embraced the two, expressing the prohibition in these words, "Be not conformed to this world," and the command in these, "But be ye transformed by the renewing of your mind." The former falls under the negative precept, not to covet; the latter under the positive one, to love. The one has reference to continence, the other to righteousness. The one enjoins avoidance of evil; the other, pursuit of good. By eschewing covetousness, we put off the old man, and by showing love we put on the new. But no man can be continent unless God endow him with the gift; nor is God's love shed abroad in our hearts by our own selves, but by the Holy Ghost that is given to us. This, however, takes place day after day in those who advance by willing, believing, and praying, and who, "forgetting those things which are behind, reach forth unto those things which are before." For the reason why the law inculcates all these precepts is, that when a man has failed in fulfilling them, he may not be swollen with pride, and so exalt himself, but may in very weariness betake himself to grace. Thus, the law fulfils its office as "schoolmaster," so terrifying the man as "to lead him to Christ," to give Him his love.

Chapter VI. — (12.) The Twelfth Breviate.

XII. "Again the question arises," he says, "how it is that man is unable to be without sin, —by his will, or by nature? If by nature, it is not sin; if by his will, then will can very easily be changed by will." We answer by reminding him how he ought to reflect on the extreme presumption of saying—not simply that it is possible (for this no doubt is undeniable, when God's grace comes in aid), but—that it is "very easy" for will to be changed by will; whereas the apostle says, "The flesh lusted against the spirit, and the spirit against the flesh: and these are contrary the one to the other; so that ye do not the things that ye would." He does not say, "These are contrary the one to the other, so that ye will not do the things that ye can," but, "so that ye do not the things that ye would." How happens it, then, that the lust of the flesh which of course is culpable and corrupt, and is nothing else than the desire for sin, as to which the same apostle instructs us not to let it "reign in our mortal body;" by which expression he shows us plainly enough that that must have an existence in our mortal body which must not be permitted to hold a dominion in it;—how happens it, I say, that such lust of the flesh has not been changed by that will, which the apostle clearly implied the existence of in his words, "So that ye do not the things that ye would," if so be that the will can so easily be changed by will? Not that we, indeed, by this argument throw the blame upon the nature either of the soul or of the body, which God created, and which is wholly good; but we say that it, having been corrupted by its own will, cannot be made whole without the grace of God.

(13.) The Thirteenth Breviate.

XIII. "The next question we have to ask," says he, "is this: If man cannot be without sin, whose fault is it, — man's own, or some one's else? If man's own, in what way is it his fault if he is not that which he is unable to be?" We reply, that it is man's fault that he is not without sin on this account, because it has by man's sole will come to pass that he has come into such a necessity as cannot be overcome by man's sole will.

(14.) The Fourteenth Breviate.

XIV. "Again the question must be asked," he says, "If man's nature is good, as nobody but Marcion or Manichæus will venture to deny, in what way is it good if it is impossible for it to be free from evil? For that all sin is evil who can gainsay?" We answer, that man's nature is both good, and is also able to be free from evil. Therefore do we earnestly pray, "Deliver us from evil." This deliverance, indeed, is not fully wrought, so long as the soul is oppressed by the body, which is hastening to corruption. This process, however, is being effected by grace through faith, so that it may be said by and by, "O death, where is thy struggle? Where is thy sting, O death? The sting of death is sin, and the strength of sin is the law;" because the law by prohibiting sin only increases the desire for it, unless the Holy Ghost spreads abroad that love, which shall then be full and perfect, when we shall see face to face.

(15.) The Fifteenth Breviate.

XV. "And this, moreover, has to be said," he says: "God is certainly righteous; this cannot be denied. But God imputes every sin to man. This too, I suppose, must be allowed, that whatever shall not be imputed as sin is not sin. Now if there is any sin which is unavoidable, how is God said to be righteous, when He is supposed to impute to any man that which cannot be avoided?" We reply, that long ago was it declared in opposition to the proud, "Blessed is the man to whom the Lord imputed not sin." Now He does not impute it to those who say to Him in faith, "Forgive us our debts, as we forgive our debtors." And justly does He withhold this imputation, because that is just which He says: "With what measure ye mete, it shall be measured to you again." That, however, is sin in which there is either not the love which ought to be, or where the love is less than it ought to be, —whether it can be avoided by the human will or not; because when it can be avoided, the man's present will does it, but if it cannot be avoided his past will did it; and yet it can be avoided, —not, however, when the proud will is lauded, but when the humble one is assisted.

Chapter VII. — (16.) The Sixteenth Breviate.

XVI. After all these disputations, their author introduces himself in person as arguing with another, and represents himself as under examination, and as being addressed by his examiner: "Show me the man who is without sin." He answers: "I show you one who is able to be without sin." His examiner then says to him: "And who is he?" He answers: "You are the man." "But if," he adds, "you were to say, 'I, at any rate, cannot be without sin,' then you must answer me, 'Whose fault is that?' If you then were to say, 'My own fault,' you must be further asked, 'And how is it your fault, if you cannot be without sin?'" He again represents himself as under examination, and thus accosted: "Are you yourself without sin, who say that a man can be without sin?" And he answers: "Whose fault is it that I am not without sin? But if," continues he, "he had said in reply, 'The fault is your own;' then the answer would be, 'How my fault, when I am unable to be without sin?'" Now our answer to all this running argument is, that no controversy ought to have been raised between them about such words as these; because he nowhere ventures to affirm that a man (either anyone else, or himself) is without sin, but he merely said in reply that he can be, —a position which we do not ourselves deny. Only the question arises, when can he, and through whom can he? If at the present time, then by no faithful soul which is enclosed within the body of this death must this prayer be offered, or such words as these be spoken, "Forgive us our debts, as we forgive our debtors," since in holy baptism all past debts have been already forgiven. But whoever tries to persuade us that such a prayer is not proper for faithful members of Christ, does in fact acknowledge nothing else than that he is not himself a Christian. If, again, it is through himself that a man can live without sin, then did Christ die in vain. But "Christ is not dead in vain." No man, therefore, can be without sin, even if he wish it, unless he be assisted by the grace of God through our Lord Jesus Christ. And that this perfection may be attained, there is even now a training carried on in growing [Christians,] and there will be by all means a completion made, after the conflict with death is spent, and love, which is now cherished by the operation of faith and hope, shall be perfected in the fruition of sight and possession.

Chapter VIII. — (17.) It is One Thing to Depart from the Body, Another Thing to Be Liberated from the Body of This Death.

He next proposes to establish his point by the testimony of Holy Scripture. Let us carefully observe what kind of defense he makes. "There are passages," says he, "which prove that man is commanded to be without sin." Now our answer to this is: Whether such commands are given is not at all the point in question, for the fact is clear enough; but whether the thing which is evidently commanded be itself at all possible of accomplishment in the body of this death, wherein "the flesh lusted against the spirit, and the spirit against the flesh, so that we cannot do the things that we would." Now from this body of death not everyone is liberated who ends the present life, but only he who in this life has received grace, and given proof of not receiving it in vain by spending his days in good works. For it is plainly one thing to depart from the body, which all men are obliged to do in the last day of their present life, and another to be delivered from the body of this death, —which God's grace alone, through our Lord Jesus Christ, imparts to His faithful saints. It is after this life, indeed, that the reward of perfection is bestowed, but only upon those by whom in their present life has been acquired the merit of such a recompense. For no one, after going hence, shall arrive at fulness of righteousness, unless, whilst here, he shall have run his course by hungering and thirsting after it. "Blessed are they which do hunger and thirst after righteousness; for they shall be filled."

(18.) The Righteousness of This Life Comprehended in Three Parts, —Fasting, Almsgiving, and Prayer.

As long, then, as we are "absent from the Lord, we walk by faith, not by sight;" whence it is said, "The just shall live by faith." Our righteousness in this pilgrimage is this—that we press forward to that perfect and full righteousness in which there shall be perfect and full love in the sight of His glory; and that now we hold to the rectitude and perfection of our course, by "keeping under our body and bringing it into subjection," by doing our alms cheerfully and heartily, while bestowing kindnesses and forgiving the trespasses which have been committed against us, and by "continuing instant in prayer;"—and doing all this with sound doctrine, whereon are built a right faith, a firm hope, and a pure charity. This is now our righteousness, in which we pass through our course hungering and thirsting after the perfect and full righteousness, in order that we may hereafter be satisfied therewith. Therefore, our Lord in the Gospel (after saying, "Take heed that ye do not your righteousness before men, to be seen of them,") in order that we should not measure our course of life by the limit of human glory, declared in his exposition of righteousness itself that there is none except there be these three, —fasting, alms, prayers. Now in the fasting He indicates the entire subjugation of the body; in the alms, all kindness of will and deed, either by giving or forgiving; and in prayers He implies all the rules of a holy desire. So that, although by the subjugation of the body a check is given to that concupiscence, which ought not only to be bridled but to be put altogether out of existence (and which will not be found at all in that state of perfect righteousness, where sin shall be absolutely excluded), —yet it often exerts its immoderate desire even in the use of things which are allowable and right. In that real beneficence in which the just man consults his neighbor's welfare, things are sometimes done which are prejudicial, although it was thought that they would be advantageous. Sometimes, too, through infirmity, when the amount of the kindness and trouble which is expended either falls short of the necessities of the objects, or is of little use under the circumstances, then there steals over us a disappointment which tarnishes that "cheerfulness" which secures to the "giver" the approbation of God. This trail of sadness, however, is the greater or the less, as each man has made more or less progress in his kindly purposes. If, then, these considerations, and such as these, be duly weighed, we are only right when we say in our prayers, "Forgive us our debts, as we also forgive our debtors." But what we say in our prayers we must carry into act, even to loving our very enemies; or if anyone who is still a babe in Christ fails as yet to reach this point, he must at any rate, whenever one who has trespassed against him repents and craves his pardon, exercise forgiveness from the bottom of his heart, if he would have his heavenly Father listen to his prayer.

(19.) The Commandment of Love Shall Be Perfectly Fulfilled in the Life to Come.

And in this prayer, unless we choose to be contentious, there is placed before our view a mirror of sufficient brightness in which to behold the life of the righteous, who live by faith, and finish their course, although they are not without sin. Therefore they say, "Forgive us," because they have not yet arrived at the end of their course. Hence the apostle says, "Not as if I had already attained, either were already perfect. . .Brethren, I count not myself to have apprehended: but this one thing I do, forgetting those things which are behind, and reaching forth unto those things which are before, I press toward the mark, for the prize of the high calling of God in Christ Jesus. Let us therefore, as many as be perfect, be thus minded." In other words, let us, as many as are running perfectly, be thus resolved, that, being not yet perfected, we pursue our course to perfection along the way by which we have thus far run perfectly, in order that "when that which is perfect is come, then that which is in part may be done away;" that is, may cease to be but in part any longer, but become whole and complete. For to faith and hope shall succeed at once the very substance itself, no longer to be believed in and hoped for, but to be seen and grasped. Love, however, which is the greatest among the three, is not to be superseded, but increased and fulfilled, —contemplating in full vision what it used to see by faith, and acquiring in actual fruition what it once only embraced in hope. Then in all this plenitude of charity will be fulfilled the commandment, "Thou shalt love the Lord thy God with all thine heart, and with all thy soul, and with all thy mind." For while there remains any remnant of the lust of the flesh, to be kept in check by the rein of continence, God is by no means loved with all one's soul. For the flesh does not lust without the soul; although it is the flesh which is said to lust, because the soul lusts carnally. In that perfect state the just man shall live absolutely without any sin, since there will be in his members no law warring against the law of his mind, but wholly will he love God, with all his heart, with all his soul, and with all his mind which is the first and chief commandment. For why should not such perfection be enjoined on man, although in this life nobody may attain to it? For we do not rightly run if we do not know whether we are to run. But how could it be known, unless it were pointed out in precepts? Let us therefore "so run that we may obtain." For all who run rightly will obtain, —not as in the contest of the theatre, where all indeed run, but only one wins the prize. Let us run, believing, hoping, longing; let us run, subjugating the body, cheerfully and heartily doing alms, —in giving kindnesses and forgiving injuries, praying that our strength may be helped as we run; and let us so listen to the commandments which urge us to perfection, as not to neglect running towards the fulness of love.

Chapter IX. — (20.) Who May Be Said to Walk Without Spot; Damnable and Venial Sins.

Having premised these remarks, let us carefully attend to the passages which he whom we are answering has produced, as if we ourselves had quoted them. "In Deuteronomy, 'Thou shalt be perfect before the Lord thy God.' Again, in the same book, 'There shall be not an imperfect man among the sons of Israel.' In like manner the Savior says in the Gospel, Be ye perfect, even as your Father which is in heaven is perfect.' So the apostle, in his second Epistle to the Corinthians, says: 'Finally, brethren, farewell. Be perfect.' Again, to the Colossians he writes: 'Warning every man, and teaching every man in all wisdom, that we may present every man perfect in Christ.' And so to the Philippians: 'Do all things without murmurings and disputing, that ye may be blameless, and harmless, as the immaculate sons of God.' In like manner to the Ephesians he writes: 'Blessed be the God and father of our Lord Jesus Christ, who hath blessed us with all spiritual blessings in heavenly places in Christ; according as He hath chosen us in Him before the foundation of the world, that we should be holy and blameless before Him.' Then again to the Colossians he says in another passage: 'And you, that were sometime alienated, and enemies in your mind by wicked works, yet now hath He reconciled in the body of His flesh through death; present yourselves holy and unblameable and unreproveable in His sight.' In the same strain, he says to the Ephesians: 'That He might present to Himself a glorious Church, not having spot, or wrinkle, or any such thing but that it should be holy and without blemish.' So, in his first Epistle to the Corinthians he says 'Be ye sober, and righteous, and sin not.' So again in the Epistle of St. Peter it is written: 'Wherefore gird up the loins of your mind, be sober, and hope to the end, for the grace that is offered to you: . . . as obedient children, not fashioning yourselves according to the former lusts in your ignorance: but as He who hath called you is holy, so be ye holy in all manner of conversation; because it is written, Be ye holy; for I am holy.' Whence blessed David likewise says: 'O Lord, who shall sojourn in Thy tabernacle, or who shall rest on Thy holy mountain? He that walks without blame, and works righteousness.' And in another passage: 'I shall be blameless with Him.' And yet again: 'Blessed are the blameless in the way, who walk in the law of the Lord.' To the same effect it is written in Solomon: 'The Lord loveth holy hearts, and all they that are blameless are acceptable unto Him.'" Now some of these passages exhort men who are running their course that they run perfectly; others refer to the end thereof, that men may reach forward to it as they run. He, however, is not unreasonably said to walk blamelessly, not who has already reached the end of his journey, but who is pressing on towards the end in a blameless manner, free from damnable sins, and at the same time not neglecting to cleanse by almsgiving such sins as are venial. For the way in which we walk, that is, the road by which we reach perfection, is cleansed by clean prayer.

That, however, is a clean prayer in which we say in truth, "Forgive us, as we ourselves forgive." So that, as there is nothing censured when blame is not imputed, we may hold on our course to perfection without censure, in a word, blamelessly; and in this perfect state, when we arrive at it at last, we shall find that there is absolutely nothing which requires cleansing by forgiveness.

Chapter X.— (21.) To Whom God's Commandments are Grievous; And to Whom, Not. Why Scripture Says that God's Commandments are Not Grievous; A Commandment is a Proof of the Freedom Of Man's Will; Prayer is a Proof of Grace.

He next quotes passages to show that God's commandments are not grievous. But who can be ignorant of the fact that, since the generic commandment is love (for "the end of the commandment is love," and "love is the fulfilling of the law"), whatever is accomplished by the operation of love, and not of fear, is not grievous? They, however, are oppressed by the commandments of God, who try to fulfil them by fearing. "But perfect love casted out fear;" and, in respect of the burden of the commandment, it not only takes off the pressure of its heavy weight, but it actually lifts it up as if on wings. In order, however, that this love may be possessed, even as far as it can possibly be possessed in the body of this death, the determination of will avails but little, unless it be helped by God's grace through our Lord Jesus Christ. For as it must again and again be stated, it is "shed abroad in our hearts," not by our own selves, but "by the Holy Ghost which is given unto us." And for no other reason does Holy Scripture insist on the truth that God's commandments are not grievous, than this, that the soul which finds them grievous may understand that it has not yet received those resources which make the Lord's commandments to be such as they are commended to us as being, even gentle and pleasant; and that it may pray with groaning of the will to obtain the gift of facility. For the man who says, "Let my heart be blameless;" and, "Order Thou my steps according to Thy word: and let not any iniquity have dominion over me;" and, "Thy will be done in earth, as it is in heaven;" and, "Lead us not into temptation;" and other prayers of a like purport, which it would be too long to particularize, does in effect offer up a prayer for ability to keep God's commandments. Neither, indeed, on the one hand, would any injunctions be laid upon us to keep them, if our own will had nothing to do in the matter; nor, on the other hand, would there be any room for prayer, if our will were alone sufficient. God's commandments, therefore, are commended to us as being not grievous, in order that he to whom they are grievous may understand that he has not as yet received the gift which removes their grievousness; and that he may not think that he is really performing them, when he so keeps them that they are grievous to him. For it is a cheerful giver whom God loves. Nevertheless, when a man finds God's commandments grievous, let him not be broken down by despair; let him rather oblige himself to seek, to ask, and to knock.

(22.) Passages to Show that God's

Commandments are Not Grievous.

He afterwards adduces those passages which represent God as recommending His own commandments as not grievous: let us now attend to their testimony. "Because," says he, "God's commandments are not only not impossible, but they are not even grievous. In Deuteronomy: 'The Lord thy God will again turn and rejoice over thee for good, as He rejoiced over thy fathers, if ye shall hearken to the voice of the Lord your God, to keep His commandments, and His ordinances, and His judgments, written in the book of this law; if thou turn to the Lord thy God with all thine heart, and with all thy soul. For this command, which I give thee this day, is not grievous, neither is it far from thee: it is not in heaven, that thou shouldest say, Who will ascend into heaven, and obtain it for us, that we may hear and do it? neither is it beyond the sea, that thou shouldest say, Who will cross over the sea, and obtain it for us, that we may hear and do it? The word is nigh thee, in thy mouth, and in thine heart, and in thine hands to do it.' In the Gospel likewise the Lord says: 'Come unto me, all ye that labor and are heavy laden, and I will give you rest. Take my yoke upon you, and learn of me; for I am meek and lowly in heart: and ye shall find rest unto your souls. For my yoke is easy, and my burden is light.' So also in the Epistle of Saint John it is written: 'This is the love of God, that we keep His commandments: and His commandments are not grievous.'" On hearing these testimonies out of the law, and the gospel, and the epistles, let us be built up unto that grace which those persons do not understand, who, "being ignorant of God's righteousness, and wishing to establish their own righteousness, have not submitted themselves unto the righteousness of God." For, if they understand not the passage of Deuteronomy in the sense that the Apostle Paul quoted it,—that "with the heart men believe unto righteousness, and with their mouth make confession unto salvation;" since "they that be whole need not a physician, but they that are sick,"—they certainly ought (by that very passage of the Apostle John which he quoted last to this effect: "This is the love of God, that we keep His commandments; and His commandments are not grievous") to be admonished that God's commandment is not grievous to the love of God, which is shed abroad in our hearts only by the Holy Ghost, not by the determination of man's will by attributing to which more than they ought, they are ignorant of God's righteousness. This love, however, shall then be made perfect, when all fear of punishment shall be cut off.

Chapter XI. — (23.) Passages of Scripture Which, When Objected Against Him by the Catholics, Cœlestius Endeavors to Elude by Other Passages: the First Passage.

After this he adduced the passages which are usually quoted against them. He does not attempt to explain these passages, but, by quoting what seem to be contrary ones, he has entangled the questions more tightly. "For," says he, "there are passages of Scripture which are in opposition to those who ignorantly suppose that they are able to destroy the liberty of the will, or the possibility of not sinning, by the authority of Scripture. For," he adds, "they are in the habit of quoting against us what holy Job said: 'Who is pure from uncleanness? Not one; even if he be an infant of only one day upon the earth.'" Then he proceeds to give a sort of answer to this passage by help of other quotations; as when Job himself said: "For although I am a righteous and blameless man, I have become a subject for mockery,"—not understanding that a man may be called righteous, who has gone so far towards perfection in righteousness as to be very near it; and this we do not deny to have been in the power of many even in this life, when they walk in it by faith.

(24.) To Be Without Sin, and to Be Without Blame—How Differing.

The same thing is affirmed in another passage, which he has quoted immediately afterwards, as spoken by the same Job: "Behold, I am very near my judgment, and I know that I shall be found righteous." Now this is the judgment of which it is said in another scripture: "And He shall bring forth thy righteousness as the light, and thy judgment as the noonday." But he does not say, I am already there; but, "I am very near." If, indeed, the judgment of his which he meant was not that which he would himself exercise, but that whereby he was to be judged at the last day, then in such judgment all will be found righteous who with sincerity pray: "Forgive us our debts, as we forgive our debtors." For it is through this forgiveness that they will be found righteous; on this account that whatever sins they have here incurred, they have blotted out by their deeds of charity. Whence the Lord says: "Give alms; and, behold, all things are clean unto you." For in the end, it shall be said to the righteous, when about to enter into the promised kingdom: "I was a hungered, and ye gave me meat," and so forth. However, it is one thing to be without sin, which in this life can only be predicated of the Only-begotten, and another thing to be without accusation, which might be said of many just persons even in the present life; for there is a certain measure of a good life, according to which even in this human intercourse there could no just accusation be possibly laid against him. For who can justly accuse the man who wishes evil to no one, and who faithfully does good to all he can, and never cherishes a wish to avenge himself on any man who does him wrong, so that he can truly say, "As we forgive our debtors?" And yet by the very fact that he truly says, "Forgive, as we also forgive," he plainly admits that he is not without sin.

(25.) Hence the force of the statement: "There was no injustice in my hands, but my prayer was pure." For the purity of his prayer arose from this circumstance, that it was not improper for him to ask forgiveness in prayer, when he really bestowed forgiveness himself.

(26.) Why Job Was So Great a Sufferer.

And when he says concerning the Lord, "For many bruises hath He inflicted upon me without a cause," observe that his words are not, He hath inflicted none with a cause; but, "many without a cause." For it was not because of his manifold sins that these many bruises were inflicted on him, but in order to make trial of his patience. For because his sins, indeed, without which, as he acknowledges in another passage, he was certainly not, he yet judges that he ought to have suffered less.

(27.) Who May Be Said to Keep the Ways of the Lord; What It is to Decline and Depart from the Ways of the Lord.

Then again, as for what he says, "For I have kept His ways, and have not turned aside from His commandments, nor will I depart from them;" he has kept God's ways who does not so turn aside as to forsake them, but makes progress by running his course therein; although, weak as he is, he sometimes stumbles or falls, onward, however, he still goes, sinning less and less until he reaches the perfect state in which he will sin no more. For in no other way could he make progress, except by keeping His ways. The man, indeed, who declines from these and becomes an apostate at last, is certainly not he who, although he has sin, yet never ceases to persevere in fighting against it until he arrives at the home where there shall remain no more conflict with death. Well now, it is in our present struggle therewith that we are clothed with the righteousness in which we here live by faith, — clothed with it as it were with a breastplate. Judgment also we take on ourselves; and even when it is against us, we turn it round to our own behalf; for we become our own accusers and condemn our sins: whence that scripture which says, "The righteous man accuses himself at the beginning of his speech." Hence also he says: "I put on righteousness, and clothed myself with judgment like a mantle." Our vesture at present no doubt is wont to be armor for war rather than garments of peace, while concupiscence has still to be subdued; it will be different by and by, when our last enemy death shall be destroyed, and our righteousness shall be full and complete, without an enemy to molest us more.

(28.) When Our Heart May Be Said Not to Reproach Us; When Good is to Be Perfected.

Furthermore, concerning these words of Job, "My heart shall not reproach me in all my life," we remark, that it is in this present life of ours, in which we live by faith, that our heart does not reproach us, if the same faith whereby we believe unto righteousness does not neglect to rebuke our sin. On this principle the apostle says: "The good that I would I do not; but the evil which I would not, that I do." Now it is a good thing to avoid concupiscence, and this good the just man would, who lives by faith; and still he does what he hates, because he has concupiscence, although "he goes not after his lusts;" if he has done this, he has himself at that time really done it, so as to yield to, and acquiesce in, and obey the desire of sin. His heart then reproaches him, because it reproaches himself, and not his sin which dwelleth in him. But whensoever he suffers not sin to reign in his mortal body to obey it in the lusts thereof, and yields not his members as instruments of unrighteousness unto sin, sin no doubt is present in his members, but it does not reign, because its desires are not obeyed. Therefore, while he does that which he would not, —in other words, while he wishes not to lust, but still lusts, —he consents to the law that it is good: for what the law would, that he also wishes; because it is his desire not to indulge concupiscence, and the law expressly says, "Thou shalt not covet." Now in that he wishes what the law also would have done, he no doubt consents to the law: but still he lusts, because he is not without sin; it is, however, no longer himself that does the thing, but the sin which dwells within him. Hence it is that "his heart does not reproach him in all his life;" that is, in his faith, because the just man lives by faith, so that his faith is his very life. He knows, to be sure, that in himself dwells nothing good, —even in his flesh, which is the dwelling-place of sin. By not consenting, however, to it, he lives by faith, wherewith he also calls upon God to help him in his contest against sin. Moreover, there is present to him to will that no sin at all should be in him, but then how to perfect this good is not present. It is not the mere "doing" of a good thing that is not present to him, but the "perfecting" of it. For in this, that he yields no consent, he does good; he does good again, in this, that he hates his own lust; he does good also, in this, that he does not cease to give alms; and in this, that he forgives the man who sins against him, he does good; and in this, that he asks forgiveness for his own trespasses,—sincerely avowing in his petition that he also forgives those who trespass against himself, and praying that he may not be led into temptation, but be delivered from evil,—he does good. But how to perfect the good is not present to him; it will be, however, in that final state, when the concupiscence which dwells in his members shall exist no more. His heart, therefore, does not reproach him, when it reproaches the sin which dwells in his members; nor can it reproach unbelief in him. Thus "in all his life,"—that is, in his faith, —he is neither reproached by his own heart, nor convinced of not being without sin. And Job himself acknowledges this concerning himself, when he says, "Not one of my sins hath escaped Thee; Thou hast sealed up my transgressions in a bag, and marked if I have done iniquity unawares." With regard, then, to the passages which he has adduced from the book of holy Job, we have shown to the best of our ability in what sense they ought to be taken. He, however, has failed to explain the meaning of the words which he has himself quoted from the same Job: "Who then is pure from uncleanness? Not one; even if he be an infant of only one day upon the earth."

Chapter XII. — (29.) The Second Passage. Who May Be Said to Abstain from Every Evil Thing.

"They are in the habit of next quoting," says he, "the passage: 'Every man is a liar.'" But here again he offers no solution of words which are quoted against himself even by himself; all he does is to mention other apparently opposite passages before persons who are unacquainted with the sacred Scriptures, and thus to cast the word of God into conflict. This is what he says: "We tell them in answer, how in the book of Numbers it is said, 'Man is true.' While of holy Job this eulogy is read: 'There was a certain man in the land of Ausis, whose name was Job; that man was true, blameless, righteous, and godly, abstaining from every evil thing.'" I am surprised that he has brought forward this passage, which says that Job "abstained from every evil thing," wishing it to mean "abstained from every sin;" because he has argued already that sin is not a thing, but an act. Let him recollect that, even if it is an act, it may still be called a thing. That man, however, abstains from every evil thing, who either never consents to the sin, which is always with him, or, if sometimes hard pressed by it, is never oppressed by it; just as the wrestling champion, who, although he is sometimes caught in a fierce grapple, does not for all that lose the prowess which constitutes him the better man. We read, indeed, of a man without blame, of one without accusation; but we never read of one without sin, except the Son of man, who is also the only-begotten Son of God.

(30.) "Every Man is a Liar," Owing to Himself Alone; But "Every Man is True," By Help Only of the Grace of God.

"Moreover," says he, "in Job himself it is said: 'And he maintained the miracle of a true man.' Again we read in Solomon, touching wisdom: 'Men that are liars cannot remember her, but men of truth shall be found in her.' Again in the Apocalypse: 'And in their mouth was found no guile, for they are without fault.'" To all these statements we reply with a reminder to our opponents, of how a man may be called true, through the grace and truth of God, who is in himself without doubt a liar. Whence it is said: "Every man is a liar." As for the passage also which he has quoted about Wisdom, when it is said, "Men of truth shall be found in her," we must observe that it is undoubtedly not "in her," but in themselves that men shall be found liars. Just as in another passage: "Ye were sometimes darkness, but now are ye light in the Lord,"— when he said, "Ye were darkness," he did not add, "in the Lord;" but after saying, "Ye are now light," he expressly added the phrase, "in the Lord," for they could not possibly be "light" in themselves; in order that "he who gloried may glory in the Lord." The "faultless" ones, indeed, in the Apocalypse, are so called because "no guile was found in their mouth." They did not say they had no sin: if they had said this, they would deceive themselves, and the truth would not be in them; and if the truth were not in them, guile and untruth would be found in their mouth. If, however, to avoid envy, they said they were not without sin, although they were sinless, then this very insincerity would be a lie, and the character given of them would be untrue: "In their mouth was found no guile." Hence indeed "they are without fault;" for as they have forgiven those who have done them wrong, so are they purified by God's forgiveness of themselves. Observe now how we have to the best of our power explained in what sense the quotations he has in his own behalf advanced ought to be understood. But how the passage, "Every man is a liar," is to be interpreted, he on his part has altogether omitted to explain; nor is an explanation within his power, without a correction of the error which makes him believe that man can be true without the help of God's grace, and merely by virtue of his own free will.

Chapter XIII. — (31.) The Third Passage. It is One Thing to Depart, and Another Thing to Have Departed, from All Sin. "There is None that Doeth Good,"—Of Whom This is to Be Understood.

He has likewise propounded another question, as we shall proceed to show, but has failed to solve it; nay, he has rather rendered it more difficult, by first stating the testimony that had been quoted against him: "There is none that doeth good, no, not one;" and then resorting to seemingly contrary passages to show that there are persons who do good. This he succeeded, no doubt, in doing. It is, however, one thing for a man not to do good, and another thing not to be without sin, although he at the same time may do many good things. The passages, therefore, which he adduces are not really contrary to the statement that no person is without sin in this life. He does not, for his own part, explain in what sense it is declared that "there is none that doeth good, no, not one." These are his words: "Holy David indeed says, 'Hope thou in the Lord and be doing good.'" But this is a precept, and not an accomplished fact; and such a precept as is never kept by those of whom it is said, "There is none that doeth good, no, not one." He adds: "Holy Tobit also said, 'Fear not, my son, that we must endure poverty; we shall have many blessings if we fear God, and depart from all sin, and do that which is good.'" Most true indeed it is, that man shall have many blessings when he shall have departed from all sin. Then no evil shall betide him; nor shall he have need of the prayer, "Deliver us from evil." Although even now every man who progresses, advancing ever with an upright purpose, departs from all sin, and becomes further removed from it as he approaches nearer to the fulness and perfection of the righteous state; because even concupiscence itself, which is sin dwelling in our flesh, never ceases to diminish in those who are making progress, although it still remains in their mortal members. It is one thing, therefore, to depart from all sin, —a process which is even now in operation, —and another thing to have departed from all sin, which shall happen in the state of future perfection. But still, even he who has departed already from evil, and is continuing to do so, must be allowed to be a doer of good. How then is it said, in the passage which he has quoted and left unsolved, "There is none that doeth good, no, not one," unless that the Psalmist there censures someone nation, amongst whom there was not a man that did good, wishing to remain "children of men," and not sons of God, by whose grace man becomes good, in order to do good? For we must suppose the Psalmist here to mean that "good" which he describes in the context, saying, "God looked down from heaven upon the children of men, to see if there were any that did understand, and seek God." Such good then as this, seeking after God, there was not a man found who pursued it, no, not one; but this was in that class of men which is predestinated to destruction. It was upon such that God looked down in His foreknowledge, and passed sentence.

Chapter XIV. — (32.) The Fourth Passage. In What Sense God Only is Good. With God to Be Good and to Be Himself are the Same Thing.

"They likewise," says he, "quote what the Savior says: 'Why calls thou me good? There is none good save one, that is, God?'" This statement, however, he makes no attempt whatever to explain; all he does is to oppose to it sundry other passages which seem to contradict it, which he adduces to show that man, too, is good. Here are his remarks: "We must answer this text with another, in which the same Lord says, 'A good man out of the good treasure of his heart brings forth good things.' And again: 'He makes His sun to rise on the good and on the evil.' Then in another passage it is written, 'For the good things are created from the beginning;' and yet again, 'They that are good shall dwell in the land.'" Now to all this we must say in answer, that the passages in question must be understood in the same sense as the former one, "There is none good, save one, that is, God." Either because all created things, although God made them very good, are yet, when compared with their Creator, not good, being in fact incapable of any comparison with Him. For in a transcendent, and yet very proper sense, He said of Himself, "I Am that I Am." The statement therefore before us, "None is good save one, that is, God," is used in some such way as that which is said of John, "He was not that light;" although the Lord calls him "a lamp," just as He says to His disciples: "Ye are the light of the world: . . .neither do men light a lamp and put it under a bushel." Still, in comparison with that light which is "the true light which lighted every man that cometh into the world," he was not light. Or else, because the very sons of God even, when compared with themselves as they shall hereafter become in their eternal perfection, are good in such a way that they still remain also evil. Although I should not have dared to say this of them (for who would be so bold as to call them evil who have God for their Father?) unless the Lord had Himself said: "If ye then, being evil, know how to give good gifts to your children, how much more shall your Father which is in heaven give good things to them that ask Him?" Of course, by applying to them the words, "your Father," He proved that they were already sons of God; and yet at the same time He did not hesitate to say that they were "evil." Your author, however, does not explain to us how they are good, whilst yet "there is none good save one, that is, God." Accordingly, the man who asked, "what good thing he was to do," was admonished to seek Him by whose grace he might be good; to whom also to be good is nothing else than to be Himself, because He is unchangeably good, and cannot be evil at all.

(33.) The Fifth Passage.

"This," says he, "is another text of theirs: 'Who will boast that he has a pure heart?'" And then he answered this with several passages, wishing to show that there can be in man a pure heart. But he omits to inform us how the passage which he reported as quoted against himself must be taken, so as to prevent Holy Scripture seeming to be opposed to itself in this text, and in the passages by which he makes his answer. We for our part indeed tell him, in answer, that the clause, "Who will boast that he has a pure heart?" is a suitable sequel to the preceding sentence, "whenever a righteous king sits upon the throne." For how great so ever a man's righteousness may be, he ought to reflect and think, lest there should be found something blameworthy, which has escaped indeed his own notice, when that righteous King shall sit upon His throne, whose cognizance no sins can possibly escape, not even those of which it is said, "Who understands his transgressions?" "When, therefore, the righteous King shall sit upon His throne, . . . who will boast that he has a pure heart? or who will boldly say that he is pure from sin?" Except perhaps those who wish to boast of their own righteousness, and not glory in the mercy of the Judge Himself.

Chapter XV. — (34.) The Opposing Passages.

And yet the passages are true which he goes on to adduce by way of answer, saying: "The Savior in the gospel declares, 'Blessed are the pure in heart; for they shall see God.' David also says, 'Who shall ascend into the hill of the Lord? or who shall stand in His holy place? He that is innocent in his hands, and pure in his heart;' and again in another passage, 'Do good, O Lord, unto those that be good and upright in heart.' So also in Solomon: 'Riches are good unto him that hath no sin on his conscience;' and again in the same book, 'Leave off from sin, and order thine hands aright, and cleanse thy heart from wickedness.' So in the Epistle of John, 'If our heart condemns us not, then have we confidence toward God; and whatsoever we ask, we shall receive of Him.'" For all this is accomplished by the will, by the exercise of faith, hope, and love; by keeping under the body; by doing alms; by forgiving injuries; by earnest prayer; by supplicating for strength to advance in our course; by sincerely saying, "Forgive us, as we also forgive others," and "Lead us not into temptation, but deliver us from evil." By this process, it is certainly brought about that our heart is cleansed, and all our sin taken away; and what the righteous King, when sitting on His throne, shall find concealed in the heart and uncleansed as yet, shall be remitted by His mercy, so that the whole shall be rendered sound and cleansed for seeing God. For "he shall have judgment without mercy, that hath showed no mercy: yet mercy triumphed against judgment." If it were not so, what hope could any of us have? "When, indeed, the righteous King shall sit upon His throne, who shall boast that he hath a pure heart, or who shall boldly say that he is pure from sin?" Then, however, through His mercy shall the righteous, being by that time fully and perfectly cleansed, shine forth like the glorious sun in the kingdom of their Father.

(35.) The Church Will Be Without Spot and Wrinkle After the Resurrection.

Then shall the Church realize, fully and perfectly, the condition of "not having spot, or wrinkle, or any such thing," because then also will it in a real sense be glorious. For inasmuch as he added the epithet "glorious," when he said, "That He might present the Church to Himself, not having spot, or wrinkle, or any such thing," he signified sufficiently when the Church will be without spot, or wrinkle, or anything of this kind, —then of course when it shall be glorious. Because it is not so much when the Church is involved in so many evils, or amidst such offences, and in so great a mixture of very evil men, and amidst the heavy reproaches of the ungodly, that we ought to say that it is glorious, because kings serve it,—a fact which only produces a more perilous and a sorer temptation;—but then shall it rather be glorious, when that event shall come to pass of which the apostle also speaks in the words, "When Christ, who is your life, shall appear, then shall ye also appear with Him in glory." For since the Lord Himself, in that form of a servant by which He united Himself as Mediator to the Church, was not glorified except by the glory of His resurrection (whence it is said, "The Spirit was not yet given, because Christ was not yet glorified"), how shall His Church be described as glorious, before its resurrection? He cleanses it, therefore, now "by the laver of the water in the word," washing away its past sins, and driving off from it the dominion of wicked angels; but then by bringing all its healthy powers to perfection, He makes it meet for that glorious state, where it shall shine without a spot or wrinkle. For "whom He did predestinate, them He also called; and whom He called, them He also justified; and whom He justified, them He also glorified." It was under this mystery, as I suppose, that that was spoken, "Behold, I cast out devils, and I do cures to-day and to-morrow, and the third day I shall be consummated," or perfected. For He said this in the person of His body, which is His Church, putting days for distinct and appointed periods, which He also signified in "the third day" in His resurrection.

(36.) The Difference Between the Upright in Heart and the Clean in Heart.

I suppose, too, that there is a difference between one who is upright in heart and one who is clean in heart. A man is upright in heart when he "reaches forward to those things which are before, forgetting those things which are behind" so as to arrive in a right course, that is, with right faith and purpose, at the perfection where he may dwell clean and pure in heart. Thus, in the psalm, the conditions ought to be severally bestowed on each separate character, where it is said, "Who shall ascend into the hill of the Lord? or who shall stand in His holy place? He that is innocent in his hands, and clean in his heart." He shall ascend, innocent in his hands, and stand, clean in his heart, —the one state in present operation, the other in its consummation. And of them should rather be understood that which is written: "Riches are good unto him that hath no sin on his conscience." Then indeed shall accrue the good, or true riches, when all poverty shall have passed away; in other words, when all infirmity shall have been removed. A man may now indeed "leave off from sin," when in his onward course he departs from it, and is renewed day by day; and he may "order his hands," and direct them to works of mercy, and "cleanse his heart from all wickedness,"—he may be so merciful that what remains may be forgiven him by free pardon. This indeed is the sound and suitable meaning, without any vain and empty boasting, of that which St. John said: "If our heart condemns us not, then have we confidence toward God. And whatsoever we ask, we shall receive of Him." The warning which he clearly has addressed to us in this passage, is to beware lest our heart should reproach us in our very prayers and petitions; that is to say, lest, when we happen to resort to this prayer, and say, "Forgive us, even as we ourselves forgive, we should have to feel compunction for not doing what we say, or should even lose boldness to utter what we fail to do, and thereby forfeit the confidence of faithful and earnest prayer.

Chapter XVI. — (37.) The Sixth Passage.

He has also adduced this passage of Scripture, which is very commonly quoted against his party: "For there is not a just man upon earth, that does good, and sins not." And he makes a pretense of answering it by other passages, —how, "the Lord says concerning holy Job, 'Hast thou considered my servant Job? For there is none like him upon earth, a man who is blameless, true, a worshipper of God, and abstaining from every evil thing.'" On this passage we have already made some remarks. But he has not even attempted to show us how, on the one hand, Job was sinless upon earth, —if the words are to bear such a sense; and, on the other hand, how that can be true which he has admitted being in the Scripture, "There is not a just man upon earth, that does good, and sins not."

Chapter XVII. — (38.) The Seventh Passage. Who May Be Called Immaculate. How It is that in God's Sight No Man is Justified.

"They also, says he, "quote the text: 'For in thy sight shall no man living be justified.'" And his affected answer to this passage amounts to nothing else than the showing how texts of Holy Scripture seem to clash with one another, whereas it is our duty rather to demonstrate their agreement. These are his words: "We must confront them with this answer, from the testimony of the evangelist concerning holy Zacharias and Elisabeth, when he says, 'And they were both righteous before God, walking in all the commandments and ordinances of the Lord blameless.'" Now both these righteous persons had, of course, read amongst these very commandments the method of cleansing their own sins. For, according to what is said in the Epistle to the Hebrews of "every high priest taken from among men," Zacharias used no doubt to offer sacrifices even for his own sins. The meaning, however, of the phrase "blameless," which is applied to him, we have already, as I suppose, sufficiently explained. "And," he adds, "the blessed apostle says, 'That we should be holy, and without blame before Him.'" This, according to him, is said that we should be so, if those persons are to be understood by "blameless" who are altogether without sin. If, however, they are "blameless" who are without blame or censure, then it is impossible for us to deny that there have been, and still are, such persons even in this present life; for it does not follow that a man is without sin because he has not a blot of accusation. Accordingly, the apostle, when selecting ministers for ordination, does not say, "If any be sinless," for he would be unable to find any such; but he says, "If any be without accusation," for such, of course, he would be able to find. But our opponent does not tell us how, in accordance with his views, we ought to understand the scripture, "For in Thy sight shall no man living be justified." The meaning of these words is plain enough, receiving as it does additional light from the preceding clause: "Enter not," says the Psalmist, "into judgment with Thy servant, for in Thy sight shall no man living be justified." It is judgment which he fears, therefore he desires that mercy which triumphs over judgment. For the meaning of the prayer, "Enter not into judgment with Thy servant," is this: "Judge me not according to Thyself," who art without sin; "for in Thy sight shall no man living be justified." This without doubt is understood as spoken of the present life, whilst the predicate "shall not be justified" has reference to that perfect state of righteousness which belongs not to this life.

Chapter XVIII. — (39.) The Eighth Passage. In What Sense He is Said Not to Sin Who is Born of God. In What Way He Who Sins Shall Not See Nor Know God.

"They also quote," says he, "this passage, "If we say that we have no sin, we deceive ourselves, and the truth is not in us." And this very clear testimony he has endeavored to meet with apparently contradictory texts, saying thus: "The same St. John in this very epistle says, 'This, however, brethren, I say, that ye sin not. Whosoever is born of God doth not commit sin; for his seed remained in him: and he cannot sin.' Also elsewhere: 'Whosoever is born of God sinned not; because his being born of God preserved him, and the evil one touched him not.' And again in another passage, when speaking of the Savior, he says: 'Since He was manifested to take away sins, whosoever abided in Him sinned not: whosoever sinned hath not seen Him, neither known Him.' And yet again: 'Beloved, now are we the sons of God; and it doth not yet appear what we shall be: but we know that, when He shall appear, we shall be like Him; for we shall see Him as He is. And every man that hath this hope towards Him purified himself, even as He is pure.'" And yet, notwithstanding the truth of all these passages, that also is true which he has adduced, without, however, offering any explanation of it: "If we say that we have no sin, we deceive ourselves, and the truth is not in us." Now it follows from the whole of this, that in so far as we are born of God we abide in Him who appeared to take away sins, that is, in Christ, and sin not,—which is simply that "the inward man is renewed day by day;" but in so far as we are born of that man "through whom sin entered into the world, and death by sin, and so death passed upon all men," we are not without sin, because we are not as yet free from his infirmity, until, by that renewal which takes place from day to day (for it is in accordance with this that we were born of God), that infirmity shall be wholly repaired, wherein we were born from the first than, and in which we are not without sin. While the remains of this infirmity abide in our inward man, however much they may be daily lessened in those who are advancing, "we deceive ourselves, and the truth is not in us, if we say that we have no sin." Now, however true it is that "whosoever sinned hath not seen Him, nor known Him," since with that vision and knowledge, which shall be realized in actual sight, no one can in this life see and know Him; yet with that vision and knowledge which come of faith, there may be many who commit sin,—even apostates themselves,—who still have believed in Him some time or other; so that of none of these could it be said, according to the vision and knowledge which as yet come of faith, that he has neither seen Him nor known Him. But I suppose it ought to be understood that it is the renewal which awaits perfection that sees and knows Him; whereas the infirmity which is destined to waste and ruin neither sees nor knows Him. And it is owing to the remains of this infirmity, of whatever amount, which remain firm in our inward man, that "we deceive ourselves, and have not the truth in us, when we say that we have no sin." Although, then, by the grace of renovation "we are the sons of God," yet because of the remains of infirmity within us "it doth not appear what we shall be; only we know that, when He shall appear, we shall be like Him, for we shall see Him as He is." Then there shall be no more sin, because no infirmity shall any longer remain within us or without us. "And every man that hath this hope towards Him purified himself, even as He is pure,"—purified himself, not indeed by himself alone, but by believing in Him, and calling on Him who sanctified His saints; which sanctification, when perfected at last (for it is at present only advancing and growing day by day), shall take away from us forever all the remains of our infirmity.

Chapter XIX— (40.) The Ninth Passage.

"This passage, too," says he, "is quoted by them: 'It is not of him that willed, nor of him that runs, but of God that showed mercy.'" And he observes that the answer to be given to them is derived from the same apostle's words in another passage: "Let him do what he will." And he adds another passage from the Epistle to Philemon, where, speaking of Onesimus, [St. Paul says]: "'Whom I would have retained with me, that in thy stead he might have ministered unto me in the bonds of the gospel. But without thy mind would I do nothing; that thy benefit should not be as it were of necessity, but willingly.' Likewise, in Deuteronomy: 'Life and death hath He set before thee, and good and evil: . . .choose thou life, that thou mayest live.' So in the book of Solomon: 'God from the beginning made man, and left him in the hand of His counsel; and He added for him commandments and precepts: if thou wilt—to perform acceptable faithfulness for the time to come, they shall save thee. He hath set fire and water before thee: stretch forth thine hand unto whether thou wilt. Before man are good and evil, and life and death; poverty and honor are from the Lord God.' So again in Isaiah we read: 'If ye be willing, and hearken unto me, ye shall eat the good of the land; but if ye be not willing, and hearken not to me, the sword shall devour you: for the mouth of the Lord hath spoken this.'" Now with all their efforts of disguise they here betray their purpose; for they plainly attempt to controvert the grace and mercy of God, which we desire to obtain whenever we offer the prayer, "Thy will be done in earth as it is in heaven;" or again this, "Lead us not into temptation, but deliver us from evil." For indeed why do we present such petitions in earnest supplication, if the result is of him that willed, and him that runs, but not of God that showed mercy? Not that the result is without our will, but that our will does not accomplish the result, unless it receive the divine assistance. Now the wholesomeness of faith is this, that it makes us "seek, that we may find; ask, that we may receive; and knock, that it may be opened to us." Whereas the man who gainsays it, does really shut the door of God's mercy against himself. I am unwilling to say more touching so important a matter, because I do better in committing it to the groans of the faithful, than to words of my own.

(41.) Specimens of Pelagian Exegesis.

But I beg of you to see what kind of objection, after all, he makes, that to him who "willed and runs" there is no necessity for God's mercy, which actually anticipates him in order that he may run, —because, forsooth, the apostle says concerning a certain person, "Let him do what he will,"—in the matter, as I suppose, which he goes on to treat, when he says, "He sinned not, let him marry!" As if indeed it should be regarded as a great matter to be willing to marry, when the subject is a labored discussion concerning the assistance of God's grace, or that it is of any great advantage to will it, unless God's providence, which governs all things, joins together the man and the woman. Or, in the case of the apostle's writing to Philemon, that "his kindness should not be as it were of necessity, but voluntary,"—as if any good act could indeed be voluntary otherwise than by God's "working in us both to will and to do of His own good pleasure." Or, when the Scripture says in Deuteronomy, "Life and death hath He set before man and good and evil," and admonishes him "to choose life;" as if, forsooth, this very admonition did not come from God's mercy, or as if there were any advantage in choosing life, unless God inspired love to make such a choice, and gave the possession of it when chosen, concerning which it is said: "For anger is in His indignation, and in His pleasure is life."

Or again, because it is said, "The commandments, if thou wilt, shall save thee,"—as if a man ought not to thank God, because he has a will to keep the commandments, since, if he wholly lacked the light of truth, it would not be possible for him to possess such a will. "Fire and water being set before him, a man stretches forth his hand towards which he pleases;" and yet higher is He who calls man to his higher vocation than any thought on man's own part, inasmuch as the beginning of correction of the heart lies in faith, even as it is written, "Thou shalt come, and pass on from the beginning of faith." Everyone makes his choice of good, "according as God hath dealt to every man the measure of faith;" and as the Prince of faith says, "No man can come to me, except the Father which hath sent me draw him." And that He spoke this about the faith which believes in Him, He subsequently explains with sufficient clearness, when He says: "The words that I speak unto you, they are spirit, and they are life; yet there are some of you that believe not. For Jesus knew from the beginning who they were that believed not, and who should betray Him. And He said, therefore said I unto you, that no man can come unto me, except it were given unto him of my Father."

(42.) God's Promises Conditional. Saints of the Old Testament Were Saved by the Grace of Christ.

He, however, thought he had discovered a great support for his cause in the prophet Isaiah; because by him God said: "If ye be willing, and hearken unto me, ye shall eat the good of the land; but if ye be not willing, and hearken not to me, the sword shall devour you: for the mouth of the Lord hath spoken this." As if the entire law were not full of conditions of this sort; or as if its commandments had been given to proud men for any other reason than that "the law was added because of transgression, until the seed should come to whom the promise was made." "It entered, therefore, that the offence might abound; but where sin abounded, grace did much more abound." In other words, That man might receive commandments, trusting as he did in his own resources, and that, failing in these and becoming a transgressor, he might ask for a deliverer and a savior; and that the fear of the law might humble him, and bring him, as a schoolmaster, to faith and grace. Thus "their weaknesses being multiplied, they hastened after;" and in order to heal them, Christ in due season came. In His grace even righteous men of old believed, and by the same grace were they holpen; so that with joy did they receive a foreknowledge of Him, and some of them even foretold His coming,—whether they were found among the people of Israel themselves, as Moses, and Joshua the son of Nun, and Samuel, and David, and other such; or outside that people, as Job; or previous to that people, as Abraham, and Noah, and all others who are either mentioned or not in Holy Scripture. "For there is but one God, and one Mediator between God and man, the man

Christ Jesus," without whose grace nobody is delivered from condemnation, whether he has derived that condemnation from him in whom all men sinned, or has afterwards aggravated it by his own iniquities.

Chapter XX. — (43.) No Man is Assisted Unless He Does Himself Also Work. Our Course is a Constant Progress.

But what is the import of the last statement which he has made: "If anyone say, 'May it possibly be that a man sin not even in word?' then the answer," says he, "which must be given is, 'Quite possible, if God so will; and God does so will, therefore it is possible.'" See how unwilling he was to say, "If God give His help, then it would be possible;" and yet the Psalmist thus addresses God: "Be Thou my helper, forsake me not;" where of course help is not sought for procuring bodily advantages and avoiding bodily evils, but for practicing and fulfilling righteousness. Hence it is that we say: "Lead us not into temptation, but deliver us from evil." Now no man is assisted unless he also himself does something; assisted, however, he is, if he prays, if he believes, if he is "called according to God's purpose;" for "whom He did foreknow, He also did predestinate to be conformed to the image of His Son, that He might be the first-born among many brethren. Moreover, whom He did predestinate, them He also called; and whom He called, them He also justified; and whom He justified, them He also glorified." We run, therefore, whenever we make advance; and our wholeness runs with us in our advance (just as a sore is said to run when the wound is in process of a sound and careful treatment), in order that we may be in every respect perfect, without any infirmity of sin whatever, —a result which God not only wishes, but even causes and helps us to accomplish. And this God's grace does, in co-operation with ourselves, through Jesus Christ our Lord, as well by commandments, sacraments, and examples, as by His Holy Spirit also; through whom there is hiddenly shed abroad in our hearts that love, "which makes intercession for us with groanings which cannot be uttered," until wholeness and salvation be perfected in us, and God be manifested to us as He will be seen in His eternal truth.

Chapter XXI. — (44.) Conclusion of the Work. In the Regenerate It is Not Concupiscence, But Consent, Which is Sin.

Whosoever, then, supposes that any man or any men (except the one Mediator between God and man) have ever lived, or are yet living in this present state, who have not needed, and do not need, forgiveness of sins, he opposes Holy Scripture, wherein it is said by the apostle: "By one man sin entered into the world, and death by sin; and so death passed upon all men, in which all have sinned." And he must needs go on to assert, with an impious contention, that there may possibly be men who are freed and saved from sin without the liberation and salvation of the one Mediator Christ. Whereas He it is who has said: "They that be whole need not a physician, but they that are sick;" "I am not come to call the righteous, but sinners to repentance." He, moreover, who says that any man, after he has received remission of sins, has ever lived in this body, or still is living, so righteously as to have no sin at all, he contradicts the Apostle John, who declares that "If we say we have no sin, we deceive ourselves, and the truth is not in us." Observe, the expression is not we had, but "we have." If, however, anybody contend that the apostle's statement concerns the sin which dwells in our mortal flesh according to the defect which was caused by the will of the first man when he sinned, and concerning which the Apostle Paul enjoins us "not" to "obey it in the lusts thereof,—so that he does not sin who altogether withholds his consent from this same indwelling sin, and so brings it to no evil work,— either in deed, or word, or thought,—although the lusting after it may be excited (which in another sense has received the name of sin, inasmuch as consenting to it would amount to sinning), but excited against our will,— he certainly is drawing subtle distinctions, and should consider what relation all this bears to the Lord's Prayer, wherein we say, "Forgive us our debts." Now, if I judge aright, it would be unnecessary to put up such a prayer as this, if we never in the least degree consented to the lusts of the before-mentioned sin, either in a slip of the tongue, or in a wanton thought; all that it would be needful to say would be, "Lead us not into temptation, but deliver us from evil." Nor could the Apostle James say: "In many things we all offend." For in truth only that man offends whom an evil concupiscence persuades, either by deception or by force, to do or say or think something which he ought to avoid, by directing his appetites or his aversions contrary to the rule of righteousness. Finally, if it be asserted that there either have been, or are in this present life, any persons, with the sole exception of our Great Head, "the Savior of His body," who are righteous, without any sin,—and this, either by not consenting to the lusts thereof, or because that must not be accounted as any sin which is such that God does not impute it to them by reason of their godly lives (although the blessedness of being without sin is a different thing from the blessedness of not having one's sin imputed to him),—I do not deem it necessary to contest the point over much. I am quite aware that some hold this opinion, whose views on the subject I have not the courage to censure, although, at the same time, I cannot defend them. But if any man says that we ought not to use the prayer, "Lead us not into temptation" (and he says as much who maintains that God's help is unnecessary to a person for the avoidance of sin, and that human will, after accepting only the law, is sufficient for the purpose), then I do not hesitate at once to affirm that such a man ought to be removed from the public ear, and to be anathematized by every mouth.

www.ingramcontent.com/pod-product-compliance
Lightning Source LLC
Chambersburg PA
CBHW052117070526
44584CB00017B/2532